WHEREAS

WHEREAS

Layli Long Soldier

Graywolf Press

This publication is made possible, in part, by the voters of Minnesota through a Minnesota State Arts Board Operating Support grant, thanks to a legislative appropriation from the arts and cultural heritage fund, and through a grant from the Wells Fargo Foundation. Significant support has also been provided by Target, the McKnight Foundation, the Amazon Literary Partnership, and other generous contributions from foundations, corporations, and individuals. To these organizations and individuals we offer our heartfelt thanks.

Published by Graywolf Press
250 Third Avenue North, Suite 600
Minneapolis, Minnesota 55401

www.graywolfpress.org

Published in the United States of America

ISBN 978-1-55597-767-2

    12   14   16   15   13   11

Library of Congress Control Number: 2016938845

Cover design: Mary Austin Speaker

Cover art: *Modest Livelihood*
        Super 16mm film transferred to HD digital file
        50:00 (silent)
        2012
        Courtesy of Brian Jungen, Duane Linklater, and Catriona Jeffries Gallery

This book is dedicated to my mother, Loevia Hockley, and my father, Daniel Long Soldier.

And with great tenderness, to my daughter, Chance Ohitika Alexie White.

Contents

No word has any special hierarchy over any other.
—ARTHUR SZE

WHEREAS

PART I

THESE BEING THE CONCERNS

Now
make room in the mouth
for grassesgrassesgrasses

Ȟe Sápa

Ȟe is a mountain as hé is a horn that comes from a shift in the river, throat to mouth. Followed by sápa, a kind of black sleek in the rise of both. Remember. Ȟe Sápa is not a black hill, not Pahá Sápa, by any name you call it. When it lives in past tense, one would say it *was* not Red Horn either; was not a rider on horse on mount and did not lead a cavalry down the river and bend, not decoy to ambush and knee buckle

to ten or twenty, perhaps every

horse face in water.

Its rank is a mountain and must live as a mountain, as a black horn does from base to black horn tip. See it as you come, you approach. To remember it, this is like gravel.

Because *drag* changes when spoken of in the past i.e. he was *dragged* or they *drug* him down
the long road, the pale rock and brown. Down dust, a knocking path. And *to drag* has a begin
point (though two are considered): begins when man is bound; begins also with one first tug.
So we take the word to our own uses and say:
it begins with his head on the ground with his hair loose
under shoulders and shirt with snaps, they're mother-of-pearl. Then begins a yank
and slide, begins his skin and scalp—
begins a break a tear, red to pink
to precious white; then begins what is
his skull, glisten of star
to bone.

This is how you see me the space in which to place me

The space in me you see

is this place

This is how to place you in the space in which to see

To see this space   see how you place me in you

Four

But
is the small way to begin.

But I could not.

As I am limited to few
words at command, such as *waŋblí.*   This
was how I wanted to begin, with the little
I know.

But could not.

Because this waŋblí, this eagle
of my imagining is not spotted, bald,
nor even a nest-eagle. It is gold,
though by definition, not ever the great Golden Eagle.
Much as the gold, by no mistake, is not ground-gold,
man-gold or nugget.   But here, it is
the gold of   light and wing   together.
Wings that do not close, but   in expanse
angle up so slightly; plunge with muscle
and stout head somewhere between
my uncle, son, father, brother.

But I failed   to begin there, with this
expanse.   Much as I failed to start
with the great point in question.
There in muscle in high inner flight always
in the plunge we fear for the falling, we buckle to wonder:
What man is expendable?

Five

Inside the wheels of wrists and hands, a white shore of book and shell.

I kneel in the hairline light of kitchen and home

where I remember the curt shuttle of eyes down, eyes up—

where I asked, *are you looking at how I've become two?*

This one combs and places a clip just above her temple, sweeping back the curtain of *why*

and *how come.* I kiss her head I say, *maybe you already know.*

Born in us, two of everything.

As in, each born to our own crown—the highest part of the natural head.

And each born to our own crown—a single power, our distinction.

But I'm dragging myself, the other me, every strand up to the surface. I remember

very little. So I plunge my ear into the hollow of a black horn,   listen to it speak.

Not one word sounds as before.

Circuitous   this

I know.

Look

the light

grass

body

whole

wholly moves

a green hill

'til   I   pull

stalk 'n root

     up
      from
black matte

soil   bed

             bead s

from grass-

             head s

one   by

one   a

part I

s p l i t

grass wires

little bulbs

silver

green

drop

lets   I

sentence

to   life

less light

quick dead

grass

          skulls

weight

less pile

dry mound

in cupped palm

what   have   I

done

what

            now

to   do

*why*thisimpulse

to

shake   the   dead

light

why   do

I   so want the   light

to

blink look

alive move

                why

do   I   so   want   it

                    still

Diction

grind the nose into a mirror

flatten the head

I to eye to I

am a door to a room I smear to enter

fog from the mouth as:

noitɔiD Diction

•

I understand *yes* I
intuit a ken
a style of speaking
or writing depend
ent upon choice
or words an accent
inflecti   on
speech-sound
quality

I cogitate I
tune up to
terms of pre
vailing stand
ards
accept
ability
enunci
ation

•

though I'm told I come from a small world a lifted paragraph from one or other book:

It took many trials before I learned how to knot my ~~sinew thread on the~~ point ~~of my finger, as I saw her do. Then~~ the ~~next~~ difficulty was in keeping my thread ~~stiffly~~ twisted, so that I could easily string ~~my beads upon it. My mother required of me~~ original designs ~~for my lessons in beading. At first I frequently ensnared many a sunny hour into working a long design.~~ Soon I learned from self-inflicted punishment ~~to refrain from drawing complex patterns, for~~ I had to finish whatever I began.

I thank Zitkála Šá as I learn to other   wise   put—

•

be
cause
when I
sweat over
diction James
Welch guides me
his angle a marginal
slope corner arrange

ment:

Plains Indi-
til 1890, when a

Wounded Knee. By
left in the continen-
on at the time the
By way of contrast,
were still coming. By
Knee, the population of
0, there would be only
reservations in the west.

their increasingly rare
ians would vent their sor-
which would give them a
bodies of the *men* who had

was a purpose, a purpose
gratuitous slaughter: It was
would be there in the world
enemy without arms or legs or
there. They wanted to live in peace

•

then I heard a poet trouble and say:

I'm a straw man for leftist critique.

•

to respond
I separate I
culture and
strand it:

straw man
a person set up
top button open
as a cover a front
amber body
for questionable enter
prise an argument
such straw hair goldly
easily refuted
I listen
to corners mouth shaded
vowel black eyes
this false stillness
an opponent rigged
defeated as a bundle
I admit I vaguely get
this world its sudden
colors aromas scratching
bombastic straw
formed into the likeness
a man a scarecrow
in rows of the growing
hard gaze back

•

leftist

a per
son on
the far
left side
of the
poli
tical
spectrum
not mere
ly lib
eral
but more
radi
cal in
support
of so
cial
change to
create
ega
litar
ian
soci
ety
its   left
ist   left

•

I
a vowel
a speaker
referring
to himherself
denotes
narrator
of literary
work writ
in first person
ic, ik, ih, ahám
a symbol for
electric
current
something
having the shape
of *i*
ego

I
denote
a vowel
ego

having the shape
of literary
referring

narrator
to himherself

something
electric
of *i*
used

current
work writ
a symbol for
ic, ik, ih, ahám
amen

Vaporative

However a light may come
through vaporative
glass pane or dry dermis
of hand winter bent
I follow that light
capacity that I have
cup-sized capture
snap-like seizure I
remember small
is less to forget
less to carry
tiny gears mini-
armature I gun
the spark light
I blink eye blink
at me to look
at me in
light eye
look twice
and I eye
alight
again.

•

When I want to write seriously I think of people like
dg for whom I wrote a long poem for whom I revised
until the poem forgot its way back troubled I let it go when
you love something let it go if it returns be a good mother
father welcome the poem open armed pull out the frying
pan grease it coat it prepare a meal
apron and kitchen sweat labor
my love my sleeves pushed
to elbows like the old days a sack
of flour and keys I push them
typography and hotcakes work
seduce a poem into believing
I can home it I can provide it
white gravy whatever the craving
poem eat and lie down full
poem rest here full don't
lift a single l
etter.

•

Strange how lying on this side works
yet on my back I grieve and turning
to my left I rewind to a child's world
so I re-turn back over to the first
position of poesis prenascent page
before any material thing makes
in this right-side peace I work most
nights I greet open-eyed delicate
pronunciations like *thank you* I thank
the empty room I still my body I work hard
not to slip a centimeter in dark work not to
interrupt my own conversation I move
my mouth as if silently reading as if a begin
ner or courting a friendship careful holding
to my chest small gifts tight 3-lettered
words in 3-word phrases I welcome in
the new new.

•

promise:

if I read you
what I wrote bear
in mind I wrote it

down only
so   *that*
I remember

•

example:

I have always wanted *opaque* to mean see-through, transparent. I'm disheartened to learn

it means the opposite. Why this instinct to assign a definition based on sound. *O-PĀK—*

I interpret O: open / P: soft / Ā: airplane or directional flight / K: cut through—translating to

that which is or allows air, airy, penetrating light, transparency. To say, you don't fool me

for a second you're opaque. To say, I'm partial to opaque objects I delight in luminosity. To say,

I'm interested in this painting on glass brightly opaque. I understand the need to define

as a need for stability. That I and you can be things, standing understood, among each other.

One word can be a poem believe it, one word can destroy a poem dare I. Say I am writing

to penetrate the opaque but I confuse it too often. I negotiate instinct when a word of lightful

meaning flips under / buries me in the work of blankets.

•

A poem about writing, *bo-ring*. Says my contemporary artistic companionate, a muscular observation and I agree. A poem about writing poems, how. Boring as it is, it asks me to do. I couldn't any other thing tonight. I sat I wrote about writing. I write I sit about writing. I'm about to write about it, writing and sitting. I will write and sit with my writing.

Defamiliarize your writing then, somebody says okay I'm not sitting then I say to somebody. I'm chewing at a funeral and. I'm nibbling my pulp knuckles. I'm watching a man with a stain on his. Pants always wrinkle in this heat, gnats and humidity. I walk to the front pew to make a lewd, joke. I regard laughter from the man in the. Pants are always honest I mean really heavy at a summer burial. Yet he doesn't ever cry, the stained man, why. When I observe nothing (unusual) I do nothing (unusual) in response. New or novel. Real lit relics on these occasions. In ritual: nobody's learning, true. And to lewd is dumb, likewise. Like the way I put up my dukes when I observe the cowboy kneel. He's praying he's asking. He doesn't see me, my gesture's futile. What am I doing here, writing. What am I doing here righting the page at funerals.

•

When I stay up late I have thoughts, continually pen-marked by the clicking-on

of an air-conditioner a cutting coolness the imbalance I hear so clearly

in critique. Yet nuance saves a line and looking / space / in the trees, I watch our dog

bounce carrying the bone of a sheep's leg. I notice the carcass and her bark: both absent.

So I learn to write around it, the meat, in wide circles to be heard. When a friend says

I believe you're privileged by being so closely under, I ruffle I ease. It's not easy.

Who'm I speaking to so often no one if not the friend. On the road to Shiprock I count

eight dust devils spiraling at once in proximity all in, a line. Then only seven.

What causes reduction in this instance? I'm tempted by the bed next to my desk, yet

the desk next to my bed "sounds" better sometimes. I don't want to hear a fiction writer say,

This is why I don't read poetry. I mean, he said it not me. Of course: influence(s). Where do I

consider myself among them she asks. A tick head burrows in the skin of a question. I glue

a coffee cup to my lips, blow the heat. The sun's not up yet the birds begin first

5:06 a.m. A signal. Lie down closely my skin to sheet and pillow now the eyes orbit

the white star of a Caps Lock light STOP don't revise a word comma semicolon or.

Head Count

In the brain I met someone educated. I spoke to this person who is educated. In the brain I spoke about unbrained things hormones and children nursing and nights without a child in the bed. Sleeping. I spoke about sleeping and in the brain I left our conversation. I went home to undress my things hormones and children and night. In the blue and undressing bed I thought of Jacob or who was it that slept with a rock as a pillow? Things I've learned in passing he laid his head on a rock at night and perhaps he would never dismiss the educated. So I think about education and that's as far / then muse the rock. Was it speckled or black, rounded or granite, saw-toothed. Does the padding of hair scalp skin and blood rested upon a rock, pulse? Surely. I feel sad for the blood bruised scalp but not for the man who was it. So much I don't know I have burned myself into a bed corner, lights out. Badly brainished.

Steady Summer

solstice grasses
see this one's a natural
anesthetic he said
when they fast
they cannot food
careful water so slide
grass needle tips
around the edges
of wounds this summer
potent
grass songs
a grass chorus moves *shhhhh*
through half-propped
windows I swallow
grass scent the solstice
makes a mind
wide makes it
oceanic blue a field in crests
swirling gyres the moving
surface fastened
in June light
here I'm certain
that certain
kinds of talk
only = pain excusing
myself I paddle
deep in high
grass waves I'm safer
outdoors than in / in those
heady grasses the mouth
loosens confesses:

I don't trust nobody
      but the land I said
I don't mean
present company
of course
you understand the grasses
hear me too always
present the grasses
confident grasses polite
command to *shhhhh*
shhh listen

      at the bottom of trailer steps
      grasshoppers power up
      plate bodies jet wings
      knock knock high
      speed thru a swaying
      green page single-spaced
      blades bold hollow
      stems *air italics*

              shhhhh

                    in midday open
                    two horseflies love-buzz
                    a simple humid meeting
                    motorized sex in place
                    then loose again
                    infinite circle eights

     shhhhh   *listen*

                down the path
                Auntie steps onto the porch
                the dog pads across wood planks
                a pause to nudge her foot

                    ssshhh

in my thoughts I hear her
two states away ask for more
mac n cheese this is good Dad
my favorite   their forks click
in blue gardens flowered borders
scrubbed secondhand plates

shhhh

this grass*shhhh*

shhhh

who have I become

Tókȟaȟ'aŋ

—to lose, to suffer loss, to be gone, lost.

Used in reply to, *what has become of it?* Found in the answer: it is light and those bubbles blown from a plastic wand to spring air into a hundred silent bursts. Or the large tree shadow, the trunk of it, with finger and limb-tips across the lawn to my toe. It is the talk we engage and the unnoticed way this shadow rears back, with black arms and twig teeth it engulfs me, your love, whole.

Is sometimes disguised as the blue water-balloon of his face in photos he sent. That is, to click the attachment, enlarge on a polished screen—to see cheek-eye-bridge-of-his-nose together, lumped as blue-purple-one.

Though it's not to wield the swift, back-forth stroke of Z, a letter wherein I found a poet's fondness for *zither* and *zeal*: a discovery I stake as my own, as if I'm man on the moon with mirror head and national flag, bouncing and weightless, clever steps into the minds of others.

But in this friend I haven't seen for years, in photos of wounds and his swollen head, is the question of why   he would click *send*.

It must be answered with an alternate word:

> < you know it as a word within a word, a seed within hull within cupped hand. It is a word that, of a sudden, waved at me from a dictionary then retreated its arms, sank back to wood and pulp depths. I flipped through guts and spine of bone-dry pages, licked fingers, hunted back and forward. The Z stroke of my eyes, heroic blades at every corner.   But I will not find it again, this countersign I failed to seize in our language for *crying in a long sustained manner, or sometimes endless.* >   Gone.

So I return to this: Tókȟaȟ'aŋ, this shell and husk, the outer word. Tókȟaȟ'aŋ, I say, in the shaking he gave me, my friend, his face, the world. Tókȟaȟ'aŋ, for why I never did hit *reply*. Tókȟaȟ'aŋ, my fingernails—dirt lined, digging. Tókȟaȟ'aŋ, guttural silence under a swing and *whump*. Tókȟaȟ'aŋ, this tire-iron to the eye.

Dilate

I.

Placed

on my chest   warm fragile

as the skin of nightfall she was   heavier than imagined   her eyes

untied from northern poles from   hard unseen   winter months

she arrived safely   mid-spring she   scrunched her brow

an up-look   to her father. There's a turning   as pupils dilate

as black vernal suns slip   into equinox. This was

we never forget her

first act.

II.

All is experienced

throu

g

h

the

body

somebody told me.

III.

Though I did not feel it

when the midwife invited   when he cut   the tie

the clean   umbilical sever when   I smiled I did   not feel it

as they took her   to wash and weigh   when I said   *you should go with her.*

Both of them gone   father and baby

in a supple empty   orange light   I listened from behind   a clock on the wall

my own face   heavy plate glass   though all experience

is ~~through~~ the body   I did not feel

my hands pull   white sheets my legs shake when   two nurses cooed

lean back   honey you are   bleeding more than expected.

Left

One

If the stanza's a room then   in the doorway I spoke soft with baby like a poet
early mornings as if the baby swirled within I syllabled *pattern*
and *paper* and *put* I tapped my breath to womb as pulse and pace teach first
yet the baby was gone by the time they checked truth is
a scopic rod pried it showed nothing my head turned to left
away from the black screen white radial lines tissue he scraped
I roll over even now my head to the left
the direction of beginnings black mark of the first letter: left, I still ask
When did I?
Where did I?

                                               Lose

baby.

Two

The night I bled was a long loop a circle night sub-earthly black and red
hands outstretched to the dark I felt my way to the sink and toilet
did it happen   then   I told him
Babe I'm bleeding we cried in the middle of the stanza
hugged as my legs shook glass tore our throats we stood
that second time unlike the first we knew what bleeding meant at the mercy
with a limited clinic closed on Sundays I explored the internet
a baby's not a fetus at eight weeks it's an embryo webbed hands eyelid folds
still I say *baby* soft like a poet two even syllables as.in. ti.ny. bo.dy. or I.was.
evenly bent in two perhaps it's just spotting I self-soothed   then
curled to the mattress my eyes splintered tree limbs red tips night window
each hour pulled downward salt waves the long ebb ocean currents

sea dregs to my bed sheets the shores my lashes I could not open
my mouth to complain in the night what more could be said
until the hard morning finally to shove this body into jeans my breath
each bump along the highway a maze of mirrors motherhood the hospital
at the sign-in window the procedural lady with a computer queried
what's my home phone cell phone where did I work what's my address
I'm bleeding I need help *now* I said then   her clicking fingers the damned phone
in the clinical cold stanza I lay on a padded table clean white paper
my legs red wet the nurse did look at me and she looked *like* me I watched her
how she held my arm empathetic us two women mouthless us two
knowing better than to say _____   was just us women a moment
quiet as snow   at the mercy   us avalanched empty

Three

Sad a baby can X long before bleeding begins often
the uterus does its cleaning through blood a methodical machine
washes itself new baby gone the mother   left
yet how do I wash clean one year later   from a dream:
a nightscape there I lined my lips red in a cloudy mirror
in a train station bathroom of all places filthy
more stained and stinking wretched by the second it was next to me
a baby wrapped in blankets on a moldy sink counter its silence
I assumed the baby dead but my conscience said *hold him*
I unwrapped to find the baby breathing as my horror as his diaper rash
open sores half-way up baby's back and a deformed nose
a loose flab of nose flesh down his fragile face
I will care for the baby I thought his nose can be fixed   then
appeared the baby's older brother standing at the sink's edge curious
and another much older brother dark haired at the door
in a train station bathroom I held a forgotten baby   left
in a bathroom where no one possibly feels washed

surrounded by three boys
needing a mother I was
their mother in a dream wherein they visited
me in a stanza where we could be nearest each other   breathing
the filth they found me in   or I would rescue them from—
which in this world is it.

Wakȟályapi

1. a word commonly used for coffee;

2. formally meaning anything that is boiled. As in to boil the white collars, to boil the binding in desire to loosen. As in the day, as it blows, will boil stiff trees. As in the boiling blood, what was not soft, traces a way through muscle to face. As in the muscle that is boiled away from the gristle. As in the pot, with the white collars and gristle. As in a boiling pot over which you are bent, you are watching. As in it will stir in your head as roots of a tree. As in the tree beneath which you left something buried. As it preferred to be buried than the fury of boiling. Or the rabbit they caught, the rabbit they boiled. As in the rabbit that came nightly, the jaw of your yard. As in the dinner you ate, the rabbit bone gnawed. As in the boiling blood you never do see. As in oleanders grown over a chain-link fence, where roots of a tree and oleander mix. Boiled and boiled in a stew, the collars and rabbits and forts in a tree. As in the rabbit in a cage outside in the sun. As in the heat, as it boiled the rabbit was dead. As in the checks and bank statements Momma boiled in the kitchen. As in the riddance of debt; a ceremony, a boiling. As in money was numbers, we would eat and not waste. As in two rabbits you remember boiled that summer: one that was caught, the other helpless in black fur—your black pet rabbit you forgot to move to the shade. As in you cried in your room child, how could you forget. As in the shade that was grace that was oleander waves. As in the bubbles in water, what comes from this boiling. As in something so light, now bloodless beneath.

Talent

my first try I made a hit it dropped from morning gray the smallest shadow both wings slipped inward mid-flight the man barked *Now* I shot again and again a third time with each arrow through the target I thought was it luck or was it skill luck or skill as the last one fell

its awkward shape made me run there pulsing on the ground I was astounded by its size a gangly white goose throbbed heaved its head my eyes dropped blood flowers opened in the snow of its neck behind my shoulder stepping down from a yellow bus

children made their way across the field I shot once more to end it quickly close range its death did I do this to spare the bird from suffering or to spare the children the sight my motives in humid cold yes my knuckles in the cold steamed bright red

because on my stomach in grass in rubber boots pockets and vest I slid along with that hunter I did as he directed from quiver my draw my black lashes in steely eyed release it felt good there it felt strong my breath in autumn was an animal there I thought did I really do this   did *I* really yet what difference is muscle is an arrow powered upward or any flight to center when I did not hear it though I clearly mouthed *poor thing poor thing poor thing*

Let

In this hour a seal upon the body   from this body the legs of tears running   in our legs
      strain of a harness   with the strain white gauze of cloud cover
      in these clouds pitch and yaw the fletching of arrow   at the arrow
      temple and brow   on our brow the twine of words   in each word
      our mother our mother   as our mothers blood and letting
      as we let the field is open   what is opened the quiet of a doe
      as a doe we eat with heads down   in our heads in our heads.

Waȟpánič̌a

I begin a line about white buttes that bend chiseled faces and click stone eyelids at night, but abandon it. Instead, I push my love into this world and mail you a summer letter. From mailbox to door, you read the commas aloud. I've become a wife of bottled water comma black liner at the lash comma and sleeves to the wrist. These weeks alone alone alone comma I pull my body to a table of empty chairs and sometimes I cannot stop the impulse to command. Alone alone I instruct *sit down* comma *eat up* comma and I write in detail to hush an echo comma the rupture of a fault line.

•

I wanted to write about waȟpánič̌a a word translated into English as *poor* comma which means more precisely *to be destitute to have nothing of one's own.* But tonight I cannot bring myself to swing a worn hammer at poverty to pound the conditions of that slow frustration. So I ask what else is there to hear? A comma instructs me to divide a sentence. To pause. The comma orders a sequence of elements the comma is caesura itself. The comma interrupts me with, quiet.

•

Father's Day comma I am not with you. I stare at a black-and-white photo of you comma my husband in a velvet shirt comma your hair tied back and your eyes on the face of our sleeping daughter. When I write comma I come closer to people I want to know comma to the language I want to speak.

•

Then a friend remarks When we speak comma question marks dashes lines little black dots don't flash or jiggle in the air before us comma in truth it's the rise and fall of the voice we must capture to mean a thing in writing. Leaning his head toward a page with some vulnerable line he adds And isn't it interesting how a comma can tip a phrase into sentimentality.

•

So I disassemble mechanics comma how to score sound music movement across the page. I watch the compassionate comma slow the singular mind of two lovers. When we cannot speak our mind the comma will cool will sigh it will lick an envelope for us. Because the tongue of a comma is detached, patient.

•

Yet I feel forced to decide if *poor* really means brittle hands dust and candy-stained mouths a neighbor girl's teeth convenience store shelves Hamburger Helper a dog's matted fur a van seat pulled to the living room floor those children playing in the carcass of a car mice on the floorboard my sweeping chill hantavirus the ripe smell a horse chewed ripped its backbone exposed the swarms of do-gooders their goodly photos the heat the cold the drunks we pass waving dollar bills again tonight a bang on the door the stories no one here can stop the urge to tell I am buried in. This is the cheapest form of poor I decide it's the oil at the surface I'm tempted to say it. But a friend asserts that anyone asserting that poverty isn't about money has never been stomach-sick over how to spend their last $3 comma on milk or gas or half for both with two children in the backseat watching. I agree to let meanings and arguments with my head thrust into the punctuation of poverty here, breathe.

•

Because wahpánica means to have *nothing* of one's own. Nothing. Yet I intend the comma to mean what we do possess so I slow myself to remember it's true a child performs best when bonded with a parent before the age of five closely comma intimately. Next to you comma our daughter closes her eyes and you rest your heads blue-black lakes comma historic glass across the pillow. She'll keep this. And if it's true that what begins as trouble will double over to the end will raise its head as a period to our sentence then I admit I perform best to the music in-between the rise and fall of the voice. Nevertheless I dig through my pockets dresser drawers bookshelves comma meticulous picking comma because I must write it to see it comma how I beg from a dictionary to learn our word for *poor* comma in a language I dare to call *my* language comma who am I. A sweeping chill my stained mouth just oil at the surface comma because I feel wahpánica I feel alone. But this is a spill-over translation for how I cannot speak my mind comma the meta-phrasal ache of being *language poor*.

Irony

I wake to
red sand I
sleep here
coral brick
hooghaan I
walk thin
rabbit brush
trails side-
step early
autumn
tarantulas
pick desert
white flowers
on full days I
inhale fe-
male rain
I stop wheels
slow sheep
bounce drop
sheep shit
across
highways
potholed
me I grass
nothing
here I meta-
grass I sleep-
walk grasses
open eyes to
blue corn sky
to cook up
stews chunks
half-chewed thru
I am this
salivating
mouth without
hands with-
out arms
bent down
shameless

face to plate to
some origin(al)
hunger aware
that I'm alone
and I alone am
the one → pushing
the head
to eat

We

Because of our breath, a troop of marching ants blows from the page. We did this together yet she doesn't like my use of *we,* the presumption. Indeed, the rude inclusion, the line in a poem

I shouldn't overstep. Black vertices, upturned address you as *you* so as to center myself to my steps toe to heel to toe, counting the lengths *we,* correct. And for you I have forgotten why

horizon, partition marked as center. Now I right and to follow the line comfortably I pace I go to retrace myself back. You and I are not ants in a line dispersed from a singular breath.

Edge

This drive along the road the bend the banks behind the wheel I am called Mommy. My name is Mommy on these drives the sand and brush the end of winter we pass. You in the rearview double buckled back center my love. Your mother's mouth has a roof your mother's mouth is a church. A hut in a field lone standing. The thatched roof has caught spark what flew from walls the spark apart from rock from stable meaning.   Large car steady at the curve palest light driest day a field of rocks we are not poor sealed in windows. You hum in the back. I do not know what to say how far to go the winter near dead as we drive you do not understand word for word the word for you is little. But you hear how it feels always. The music plays you swing your feet. And I see it I Mommy the edge but do not point do not say *look* as we pass the heads gold and blowing these dry grasses eaten in fear by man and horses.

38

Here, the sentence will be respected.

I will compose each sentence with care, by minding what the rules of writing dictate.

For example, all sentences will begin with capital letters.

Likewise, the history of the sentence will be honored by ending each one with appropriate punctuation such as a period or question mark, thus bringing the idea to (momentary) completion.

You may like to know, I do not consider this a "creative piece."

I do not regard this as a poem of great imagination or a work of fiction.

Also, historical events will not be dramatized for an "interesting" read.

Therefore, I feel most responsible to the orderly sentence; conveyor of thought.

That said, I will begin.

You may or may not have heard about the Dakota 38.

If this is the first time you've heard of it, you might wonder, "What is the Dakota 38?"

The Dakota 38 refers to thirty-eight Dakota men who were executed by hanging, under orders from President Abraham Lincoln.

To date, this is the largest "legal" mass execution in US history.

The hanging took place on December 26, 1862—the day after Christmas.

This was the *same week* that President Lincoln signed the Emancipation Proclamation.

In the preceding sentence, I italicize "same week" for emphasis.

There was a movie titled *Lincoln* about the presidency of Abraham Lincoln.

The signing of the Emancipation Proclamation was included in the film *Lincoln;* the hanging of the Dakota 38 was not.

In any case, you might be asking, "Why were thirty-eight Dakota men hung?"

As a side note, the past tense of hang is *hung,* but when referring to the capital punishment of hanging, the correct past tense is *hanged.*

So it's possible that you're asking, "Why were thirty-eight Dakota men hanged?"

They were hanged for the Sioux Uprising.

I want to tell you about the Sioux Uprising, but I don't know where to begin.

I may jump around and details will not unfold in chronological order.

Keep in mind, I am not a historian.

So I will recount facts as best as I can, given limited resources and understanding.

Before Minnesota was a state, the Minnesota region, generally speaking, was the traditional homeland for Dakota, Anishinaabeg, and Ho-Chunk people.

During the 1800s, when the US expanded territory, they "purchased" land from the Dakota people as well as the other tribes.

But another way to understand that sort of "purchase" is: Dakota leaders ceded land to the US government in exchange for money or goods, but most importantly, the safety of their people.

Some say that Dakota leaders did not understand the terms they were entering, or they never would have agreed.

Even others call the entire negotiation "trickery."

But to make whatever-it-was official and binding, the US government drew up an initial treaty.

This treaty was later replaced by another (more convenient) treaty, and then another.

I've had difficulty unraveling the terms of these treaties, given the legal speak and congressional language.

As treaties were abrogated (broken) and new treaties were drafted, one after another, the new treaties often referenced old defunct treaties, and it is a muddy, switchback trail to follow.

Although I often feel lost on this trail, I know I am not alone.

However, as best as I can put the facts together, in 1851, Dakota territory was contained to a twelve-mile by one-hundred-fifty-mile-long strip along the Minnesota River.

But just seven years later, in 1858, the northern portion was ceded (taken) and the southern portion was (conveniently) allotted, which reduced Dakota land to a stark ten-mile tract.

These amended and broken treaties are often referred to as the Minnesota Treaties.

The word *Minnesota* comes from *mni,* which means water; and *sota,* which means turbid.

Synonyms for turbid include muddy, unclear, cloudy, confused, and smoky.

Everything is in the language we use.

For example, a treaty is, essentially, a contract between two sovereign nations.

The US treaties with the Dakota Nation were legal contracts that promised money.

It could be said, this money was payment for the land the Dakota ceded; for living within assigned boundaries (a reservation); and for relinquishing rights to their vast hunting territory which, in turn, made Dakota people dependent on other means to survive: money.

The previous sentence is circular, akin to so many aspects of history.

As you may have guessed by now, the money promised in the turbid treaties did not make it into the hands of Dakota people.

In addition, local government traders would not offer credit to "Indians" to purchase food or goods.

Without money, store credit, or rights to hunt beyond their ten-mile tract of land, Dakota people began to starve.

The Dakota people were starving.

The Dakota people starved.

In the preceding sentence, the word "starved" does not need italics for emphasis.

One should read "The Dakota people starved" as a straightforward and plainly stated fact.

As a result—and without other options but to continue to starve—Dakota people retaliated.

Dakota warriors organized, struck out, and killed settlers and traders.

This revolt is called the Sioux Uprising.

Eventually, the US Cavalry came to Mnisota to confront the Uprising.

More than one thousand Dakota people were sent to prison.

As already mentioned, thirty-eight Dakota men were subsequently hanged.

After the hanging, those one thousand Dakota prisoners were released.

However, as further consequence, what remained of Dakota territory in Mnisota was dissolved (stolen).

The Dakota people had no land to return to.

This means they were exiled.

Homeless, the Dakota people of Mnisota were relocated (forced) onto reservations in South Dakota and Nebraska.

Now, every year, a group called the Dakota 38 + 2 Riders conduct a memorial horse ride from Lower Brule, South Dakota, to Mankato, Mnisota.

The Memorial Riders travel 325 miles on horseback for eighteen days, sometimes through sub-zero blizzards.

They conclude their journey on December 26, the day of the hanging.

Memorials help focus our memory on particular people or events.

Often, memorials come in the forms of plaques, statues, or gravestones.

The memorial for the Dakota 38 is not an object inscribed with words, but an *act*.

Yet, I started this piece because I was interested in writing about grasses.

So, there is one other event to include, although it's not in chronological order and we must backtrack a little.

When the Dakota people were starving, as you may remember, government traders would not extend store credit to "Indians."

One trader named Andrew Myrick is famous for his refusal to provide credit to Dakota people by saying, "If they are hungry, let them eat grass."

There are variations of Myrick's words, but they are all something to that effect.

When settlers and traders were killed during the Sioux Uprising, one of the first to be executed by the Dakota was Andrew Myrick.

When Myrick's body was found,

                                        his mouth was stuffed with grass.

I am inclined to call this act by the Dakota warriors a poem.

There's irony in their poem.

There was no text.

"Real" poems do not "really" require words.

I have italicized the previous sentence to indicate inner dialogue, a revealing moment.

But, on second thought, the words "Let them eat grass" click the gears of the poem into place.

So, we could also say, language and word choice are crucial to the poem's work.

Things are circling back again.

Sometimes, when in a circle, if I wish to exit, I must leap.

And let the body   swing.

From the platform.

                              Out

                                                      to the grasses.

PART II
WHEREAS

Introduction

On Saturday, December 19, 2009, US President Barack Obama signed the Congressional Resolution of Apology to Native Americans. No tribal leaders or official representatives were invited to witness and receive the Apology on behalf of tribal nations. President Obama never read the Apology aloud, publicly—although, for the record, Senator Sam Brownback five months later read the Apology to a gathering of five tribal leaders, though there are more than 560 federally recognized tribes in the US. The Apology was then folded into a larger, unrelated piece of legislation called the 2010 Defense Appropriations Act.

My response is directed to the Apology's delivery, as well as the language, crafting, and arrangement of the written document. I am a citizen of the United States and an enrolled member of the Oglala Sioux Tribe, meaning I am a citizen of the Oglala Lakota Nation—and in this dual citizenship, I must work, I must eat, I must art, I must mother, I must friend, I must listen, I must observe, constantly I must live.

(1) Whereas Statements

WHEREAS when offered an apology I watch each movement the shoulders
high or folding, tilt of the head both eyes down or straight through
me, I listen for cracks in knuckles or in the word choice, what is it
that I want? *To feel* and mind you I feel from the senses—I read
each muscle, I ask the strength of the gesture to move like a poem.
Expectation's a terse arm-fold, a failing noun-thing
I scold myself in the mirror for holding.

Because I learn from young poets. One sends me new work spotted
with salt crystals she metaphors as her tears. I feel her phrases,
"I say," and "Understand me," and "I wonder."

Pages are cavernous places, white at entrance, black in absorption.
Echo.

If I'm transformed by language, I am often
crouched in footnote or blazing in title.
Where in the body do I begin;

WHEREAS a friend senses what she calls cultural emptiness in a poet's work and after a reading she feels bad for feeling bad for the poet she admits. I want to respond the same could be said for me, some sticky current of Indian emptiness, I feel it not just in my poems but when I'm on drives, in conversations, or as I lie down to sleep but since this dialogue is about writing I want to be correct with my languageness. In a note following the entry for *Indian* an Oxford dictionary warns: *Do not use Indian or Red Indian to talk about American native peoples, as these terms are now outdated; use American Indian instead.* So I explain perhaps the same could be said for my work some burden of American Indian emptiness in my poems how American Indian emptiness surfaces not just on the page but often on drives, in conversations, or when I lie down to sleep. But the term American Indian parts our conversation like a hollow bloated boat that is not ours that neither my friend nor I want to board, knowing it will never take us anywhere but to rot. If the language of race is ever truly attached to emptiness whatever it is I feel now has me in the hull, head knees feet curled, I dare say, to fetal position—but better stated as the form I resort to inside the jaws of a reference;

WHEREAS at four years old I read the first chapter of the Bible aloud I was not Christian

Whereas my hair unbraided ran the length of my spine I sometimes sat on it

Whereas at the table my legs dangled I could not balance peas on my fork

Whereas I used my fingers carefully I pushed the bright green onto silver tines

Whereas you eat like a pig the lady said setting my plate on the floor

Whereas she instructed me to finish on my hands and knees she took another bite

Whereas I watched folds of pale curtains inhale and exhale a summer dance

Whereas in the breath of the afternoon room each tick of the clock

Whereas I rose and placed my eyes and tongue on a shelf above the table first

Whereas I kneeled to my plate I kneeled to the greatest questions

Whereas that moment I knew who I was whereas the moment before I swallowed;

WHEREAS I did not desire in childhood to be a part of this but desired most of all to be a part. A piece combined with others to make up a whole. Some but not all of something. In Lakota it's haŋké, a piece or part of anything. Like the creek trickling behind my aunt's house where Uncle built her a bridge to cross from bank to bank, not far from a grassy clearing with three tipis, a place to gather. She holds three-day workshops on traditional arts, young people from Kyle and Potato Creek arrive one by one eager to *part*icipate. They have the option my auntie says to sleep at home and return in the morning but by and large they'll stay and camp even during South Dakota winters. The comfort of being together. I think of Plains winds snow drifts ice and limbs the exposure and when I slide my arms into a wool coat and put my hand to the door knob, ready to brave the sub-zero dark, someone says be careful out there always consider the snow your friend. Think badly of it, snow will burn you. I walk out remembering that for millennia we have called ourselves Lakota meaning friend or ally. This relationship to the other. Some but not all, still our piece to everything;

WHEREAS I heard a noise I thought was a sneeze. At the breakfast table pushing eggs around my plate I wondered if he liked my cooking, thought about what to talk about. He pinched his fingers to the bridge of his nose, squeezed his eyes. He wiped. I often say he was a terrible drinker when I was a child I'm not afraid to say it because he's different now: sober, attentive, showered, eating. But in my childhood when things were different I rolled onto my side, my hands together as if to pray, locked between knees. When things were different I lay there for long hours, my face to the wall, blank. My eyes left me, my soldiers, my two scouts to the unseen. And because language is the immaterial I never could speak about the missing so perhaps I cried for the invisible, what I could not see, doubly. What is it to wish for the absence of nothing? There at the breakfast table as an adult, wondering what to talk about if he liked my cooking, pushing the invisible to the plate's edge I looked up to see he hadn't sneezed, he was crying. I'd never heard him cry, didn't recognize the symptoms. I turned to him when I heard him say *I'm sorry I wasn't there sorry for many things* / like that / curative voicing / an opened bundle / or medicine / or birthday wishing / my hand to his shoulder / *it's okay* I said *it's over now* I meant it / because of our faces blankly / because of a lifelong stare down / because of centuries in sorry;

WHEREAS my eyes land on the shoreline of "the arrival of Europeans in North America opened a new chapter in the history of Native Peoples." Because in others, I hate the act

of laughing when hurt injured or in cases of danger. That bitter hiding. My daughter picks up new habits from friends. She'd been running, tripped, slid on knees and palms onto asphalt.

They carried her into the kitchen, *she just fell, she's bleeding!* Deep red streams down her arms and legs, trails on white tile. I looked at her face. A smile

quivered her. A laugh, a nervous. Doing as her friends do, she braved new behavior, feigned a grin—I couldn't name it but I could spot it. *Stop, my girl. If you're hurting, cry.*

Like that. She let it out, a flood from living room to bathroom. Then a soft water pour I washed carefully light touch clean cotton to bandage. I faced her I reminded,

In our home in our family we are ourselves, real feelings. Be true. Yet I'm serious when I say I laugh reading the phrase, "opened a new chapter." I can't help my body.

I shake. The realization that it took this phrase to show. My daughter's quiver isn't new— but a deep practice very old she's watching me;

WHEREAS a new chapter in history opened with *the thunderbird* when he phoned after dinner to say he was on his way, to meet him in the morning at the Thunderbird Inn. I knew that place on the main drag many times I'd passed the peeling adobe walls its blue trimmed windows with sleeping cars in front of each door. I took the day off work and didn't make excuses whereas I worked long weeks I'd busied myself waiting for that moment anyway. On time I pulled my wheels up close swung my legs from out the car door paced my steps as if this were a normal thing. I knocked that moment I did not waste. He opened the motel door a thick figure at the threshold he stood wearing sunglasses. But in that moment I didn't waste I didn't need to see his eyes or smile lines so much as I needed his presence so I didn't hesitate to invite him to get his things to come to my house and out from a dark room my father entered.

And whereas my father's friend a Hopi painter who served in the military listened to his grandparents after his discharge they said *Start a new chapter in life don't waste a minute!* So he packed his Hopi things his Hopi youth and arms and legs that is whatever he could of his Hopiness into a car and down the highway to the city to art school it was a good time then in Native arts the 1960s. After one holiday break the bus dropped him off alone on Cerrillos Road across from that iconic spot the Thunderbird Inn just a short walk to campus the long strides he took to pursue an endeavor he says as if it were a normal thing to be an artist.

And whereas one of my students asks a visiting poet about education vaguely getting at *what is worth pursuing?* The poet suggests looking at whatever is/was missing in one's life and begin there. So many nods in the room around that table they acknowledge it too. In the missing: power.

And whereas I enrolled in the art school where my father and his Hopi friend first met a place where the college logo is a thunderbird. Whereas looking up the word *thunderbird* I find descriptors such as supernatural which I take to mean not a normal thing. Further I find the thunderbird under a chapter heading *Native American Myths and Legends.* Whereas I once attended a summer writing program and while there a lecture by a poet on Native American myths. As a student I wanted to stand up at the mic during Q and A to challenge the terms under which one applies the term *myth* not to mention *legend* but I did not because the line was long because the speaker was well-known well-respected in other words he was a legend but not a myth. I could not work myself out from under that power nor what was missing and in hesitation / the language / my supernatural chapter ended;

WHEREAS she wrote a poem about him, he is a relative of mine. She's a lauded poet, she shakes my hand. When they were young, she says, he had an episode at the Indian school. Really? I want to ask for the story. But I don't and admire how tension chisels detail into memory. I remember her hand at the plastic zipper of her vest, the sculpture of her knuckles a bone in her wrist. How much should she tell me, how much to withhold? I watch her ask her higher self. *He broke down in a way that the rest of us wanted to,* she offers. I have not finished the poem she says. Now that we've met maybe I will. I'll send you a copy if I do. Though it has not been sent, though I'll never ask for it, I imagine the episode—him, breaking down like the rest of us want to—what this looks like on the page in poem;

Periphery
not having full
story to tell
of someone else

WHEREAS I query my uneasiness with the statement, "Native Peoples are endowed by their Creator with certain unalienable rights, and among those are life, liberty, and the pursuit of happiness." I shift in my seat a needle in my back. Though "unalienable," they're rights I cannot legally claim if placed within a Whereas Statement. Meaning whatever comes after the word "Whereas" and before the semicolon in a Congressional document falls short of legal grounds, is never cause to sue the Government, the Government's courts say. Whereas I remember that abstractions such as "life," "liberty," and "happiness" rarely serve a poem, so I have learned it best not to engage these terms anyway. Yet I smash head-on into this specific differentiation: *the* Creator vs. *their* Creator. Whereas this alters my concern entirely—how do I language a collision arrived at through separation?

When in doubt I'm told, write what I know. So I peel my eye to the moment, my love of it. I wake from a dream about running I interpret as the desire to get there. Pulling back my bed sheets, I teeter down the hall to the face of a new clock in the bathroom mirror. I say, *You're old enough now to look at yourself full-on.* Whereas I set aside interrogation to see that

I cannot

syntax or poem the Creator nor differentiate one Creator from another Creator, much less. That is, mine from theirs, theirs from ours, or why a Creator-split. At the mirror, who can;

WHEREAS I shy. Away from the cliché my friend an artist "emotes" at my table. I shy. Away too I worry and second-guess. Cliché's what's lost its original effect and power through over-use over-reliance I wash the dishes. I smell the citrus scented. In ordinary tasks I can't help the thoughts that lead me elsewhere. We chat while I rinse our cups then I bubble my hands into a pigeonhole. I remember the summer I armed myself with yellow rubber gloves and a bucket of bleach to scrub an abandoned pigeon nest on our porch. My eyes stung raw my fear of mites crawling in molten feathers layers of droppings hardened cakes of white. Whereas a pigeonhole is aka a white hole the dictionary says. A white hole's known as the white   space   between words   set   too   far   apart   in   letterpress   printing   a term synonymous with pigeonhole we don't want it. Ever to say we suffer the assignment of a stagnant place in the system my friend avoids this as an artist. She convinces me. I definitely don't want it either the stigma of a place I shy. Away from admitting to her what's in my work: this location. Where I must be firmly positioned to receive an apology the spot from which to answer. Standing here I regard an index finger popping up pointing out a reminder:

> Whereas in the infancy of the United States, the founders of the Republic expressed their desire for a just relationship with the Indian tribes, as evidenced by the Northwest Ordinance enacted by Congress in 1787, which begins with the phrase, "The utmost good faith shall always be observed toward the Indians";

Because when unconvinced   from this pigeonhole and no other   I can
    bleach and scrub   forehead sweat   rubber arms   physical effort
mental force   art and shape   muscle my back   languageness   a list of moves
    to loosen the hold   *yes I can*   shake my head wag   my finger too
      at that good faith   white cake   in a white   hole
        that stained   refusal to come   clean.

WHEREAS a string-bean blue-eyed man leans back into a swig of beer work-weary lips at the dark bottle keeping cool in short sleeves and khakis he enters the discussion;

Whereas his wrist loose at the bottleneck he comes across as candid "Well, *at least* there was an Apology, that's all I can say" he offers to the circle each of them scholarly;

Whereas under starlight the fireflies wink across east coast grass I sit there painful in my silence glued to a bench in the midst of the American casual;

Whereas a subtle electricity in that low purple light I felt their eyes on my face gauging a reaction and someone's discomfort leaks out in a well-stated "Hmmm";

Whereas like a bird darting from an oncoming semi my mind races to the Apology's assertion: "While the establishment of permanent European settlements in North America did stir conflict with nearby Indian tribes, peaceful and mutually beneficial interactions also took place";

Whereas I cross my arms and raise a curled hand to my mouth as if thinking as if taking it in I allow a static quiet then choose to stand up excusing myself I leave them to unease;

Whereas I drive down the road replaying the get-together how a man and his beer bottle stated their piece and I reel at what I could have said or done better;

Whereas I could've but didn't broach the subject of "genocide" the absence of this term from the Apology and its rephrasing as "conflict" for example;

Whereas since the moment had passed I accept what's done and the knife of my conscience slices with bone-clean self-honesty;

Whereas in a stirred conflict between settlers and an Indian that night in a circle;

Whereas I struggle to confess that I didn't want to explain anything;

Whereas truthfully I wished most to kick the legs of that man's chair out from under him;

Whereas to watch him fall backward legs flailing beer stench across his chest;

Whereas I pictured it happening in cinematic slow-motion delightful;

Whereas the curled hand I raised to my mouth was a sign of indecision;

Whereas I could've done it but I didn't;

Whereas I can admit this also took place, yes, *at least;*

WHEREAS I tire. Of my effort to match the effort of the statement: "Whereas Native Peoples and non-Native settlers engaged in numerous armed conflicts in which unfortunately, both took innocent lives, including those of women and children." I tire

of engaging in numerous conflicts, tire of the word *both*. Both as a woman and a child of that Whereas. Both of words and wordplay, hunching over dictionaries. Tire of understanding weary, weakened, exhausted, reduced in strength from labor. Bored. In a Lakota dictionary, tired is watúkȟa the dictionary claims. Under this entry, I find the term watúkȟayA meaning to exhaust somebody or something, for example to tire a horse by not knowing how properly to handle it. Am I watúkȟa or do I watúkȟayA? I call my dad to ask

and double-check my findings. How do I say "tired," he responds, "bluǧo." If you want to say "really tired," it's "lila bluǧo." This is my family's way—the Oglala way—to say tired, and who knows better what tired is than *the people*. How much must I labor

to signify what's real. *Really,* I am five feet ten inches. Really, I sleep on the right side of the bed. Really, I wake after eight hours and my eyes hang as slate gray squares. Really, I am bluǧo. Really, I climb the backs of languages, ride them into exhaustion—maybe I pull the reins when I mean go. Maybe kick their sides when I want down. Does it matter. I'm lila bluǧo. Stuck, I want off. Let loose from the impulse to note: *Beware, a horse isn't a reference to my heritage;*

WHEREAS her birth signaled the responsibility as mother to teach what it is to be Lakota, therein the question: what did I know about being Lakota? Signaled panic, blood rush my embarrassment. What did I know of our language but pieces? Would I teach her to be pieces. Until a friend comforted, *don't worry, you and your daughter will learn together.* Today she stood sunlight on her shoulders lean and straight to share a song in Diné, her father's language. To sing she motions simultaneously with her hands I watch her *be* in multiple musics. At a ceremony

to honor the Diné Nation's first poet laureate, a speaker explains that each People has been given their own language to reach with. I understand reaching as active, a motion. He offers a prayer and introduction in heritage language. I listen as I reach my eyes into my hands, my hands onto my lap, my lap as the quiet page I hold my daughter in. I rock her back, forward, to the rise of other conversations

about mother tongues versus foster languages, belonging. I connect the dots. I rock in time with references to a philosopher, a master language-thinker who thought of his mother too. Mother-to-child and child-to-mother relationships. But as this philosopher's mother suffered the ill-effects of a stroke he wrote, *I asked her if she was in pain (yes) then where? [. . . she] replies to my question: I have a pain in my mother, as though she were speaking for me, both in my direction and in my place.* His mother, who spoke in his place for his pain and as herself for her own, did this as one-and-the-same. Yet he would propose understanding the word *mother* by what mother is not, the *différance.* Forward, back. I lift my feet

my toes touch ground as I'm reminded of the linguistic impossibility of identity, as if any of us can be identical ever. To whom, to what? Perhaps to Not. I hold my daughter in comfort saying *iyotanchilah michuwintku.* True, I'm never sure how to write our language on the page correctly, the written takes many forms

yet I know she understands through our motion. Rocking, in this country of so many languages where national surveys assert that Native languages are dying. Child-speakers and elder-teachers dwindle, this is public information. But her father and I don't teach in statistics, in this dying I mean. Whereas speaking, itself, is *defiance*—the closest I can come to *différance.* Whereas I confess these are numbered hours spent responding to a national apology which concerns us, my family. These hours alone to think, without. My hope: my daughter understands wholeness for what it is, not for what it's not, all of it   the pieces;

WHEREAS we ride to the airport in a van they swivel their necks and shoulders around to speak to me sugar and lilt in their voices something like nurses their nursely kindness through my hair then engage me as comrades in a fight together. Well what we want to know one lady asks is why they don't have schools *there?* Her outrage empathy her furrowed brow. There are schools *there* I reply. Grade schools high schools colleges. But why aren't there any stores *there?* There are stores *there.* Grocery stores convenience stores trading posts whatever what-have-you I explain but it's here I recognize the break. It's here we roll along the pavement into hills of conversation we share a ride we share a country but live in alternate nations and here I must tell them what they don't know or, should I? *Should I* is the moment to seize and before I know it I say Well you know Native people as in tribes as in people living over *there* are people with their own nations each with its own government and flag they rise to their own national songs and sing in their own languages, even. And by *there* I mean *here* all around us I remind them. Drifting in side-glances to whirring trees through the van windows then back to me they dig in they unearth the golden question My God how come we were never taught this in our schools? The concern and furrow. But God the slowing wheels and we lurch forward in the van's downshift and brake. Together we reach a full stop. Trapped in a helix of traffic we're late for check-in security flights our shoulders flex forward into panicked outward gazes nerves and fingers cradle our wristwatches so to answer their question now would be untimely because to really speak to it ever is, untimely. But *there* Comrades *there there* Nurses. I will remember the swing of your gold earrings. *There* your perfume around me as a fresh blanket. *There* you checked my pulse kindly. *There* the boundary of bedside manners;

WHEREAS a woman I know says she watched a news program a reporter detailed the fire a house in which five children burned perhaps their father too she doesn't recall exactly but remembers the camera on the mother's face the mother's blubbering her hiccupping and wail she leans to me she says she never knew then in those times that year this country the northern state she grew up in she was so young you see she'd never seen it before nobody talked about them she means Indians she tells me and so on and so on but that moment in front of the TV she says was like opening a box left at her door opening to see the thing inside whereas to say she learned through that mother's face can you believe it and I let her finish wanting someone to say it but she hated saying it or so she said admitting how she never knew until then they could feel;

WHEREAS the word *whereas* means it being the case that, or considering that, or while on the contrary; is a qualifying or introductory statement, a conjunction, a connector. Whereas sets the table. The cloth. The saltshakers and plates. Whereas calls me to the table. Whereas precedes and invites. I have come now. I'm seated across from a Whereas smile. Under pressure of formalities, I fidget I shake my legs. I'm not one for these smiles, Whereas I have spent my life in unholding. *What do you mean by unholding?* Whereas asks and since Whereas rarely asks, I am moved to respond, Whereas, I have learned to exist and exist without your formality, saltshakers, plates, cloth. Without the slightest conjunctions to connect me. Without an exchange of questions, without the courtesy of answers. It is mine, this unholding, so that with or without the setup, I can see the dish being served. Whereas let us bow our heads in prayer now, just enough to eat;

WHEREAS I sipped winter water cold-steeped in pine needles, I could taste it for days afterward, I taste it now. When I woke alone gray curtains burned in sunrise and down my throat to the pit, a tincture of those green needles changed me. When should I recount detail, when's it too much? My mother burrows herself for days at a time, so I listen to her. We speak about an envelope for receipts, dark roast coffee and the neighbor's staple gun I want to borrow. In the smallest things I watch the compass needle of conversation register her back to center. What has become of us, mother to her former self. Daughter to mother, present selves. Citizen to country, former and past to present or, is it a matter of *presence?* My daughter wouldn't do it when she was younger but this year she wanted to. For her birthday, an ear piercing. The needle gun hurts only for a moment, we assure her. In the old days Grandma held ice on my earlobes then punctured with a sewing needle. You'll have it easier, I affirm. She rushes through the mall to the needle chair, her smile. Eagerness, the emotion-mark of presence. I want to write something kind, as things of country and nation and nation-to-nation burn, have tattooed me. Red-enflamed-needle-marked me. Yet in the possibility of ink through a needle, the greater picture arrives through a thousand blood dots. Long ago bones were fashioned into needles. If I had my choosing I'd use this tool here, a bone needle to break the skin. To ink-inject the permanent reminder: *I'm here I'm not / numb to a single dot;*

WHEREAS my arm locked to aim on the ground I lay stretched flat deep in a game of marbles inside a canvas pouch my garden of boulders cat eyes aggies peewees I played at recess as a fifth grader as a child I played in their shadows those bodies in cuffed jeans and sneakers three boys moved in stood over me heavy breathing I squinted upward my heart whirred loud as a card in the spokes of a wheel the big-boned blondie let out a piercing "warcry" three boys together whooped and played Indian circled and stomped hands fanning their mouths I lowered my aim rose to my knees gathered my marbles within a jeering circle pink faces sweat laughter the valley sun pounded my back my scalp my dark burning hair I toted my pouch across the playground walked alone as if climbing a descending escalator useless steps to safety I entered the classroom flip top desks with metal bellies glancing outward to classmates rows of post-recess chatter fluorescent lighting side glances no one spoke not one syllable to me I steadied my empty body at the desk stowed my marbles inside a metal belly never again to lie in the dirt on my stomach never again to call this a game in America;

And whereas in my bed in a doorway of dreaming I stood holding a stack of folded blue wool black metal eyelets brass buttons a wooden spool blue thread a pack of sewing needles as if a servant pliant and waiting my forearms upturned I held the makings there I felt a summons I turn to a black-and-white photo you're seated with a canumpa and cloth across your lap I trace a horizontal scar across the bridge of your nose in your eyes mottled irises a torn surface your life on your face this mirror of our family I note a plume in your top hat down both shoulders your hair wrapped in fur strong veins pump through wrists to a soldier's hands a choker above the top button of your wool coat I know how you got that coat I search for a place even marginal to share the story this thread in the seams of our family but what's on a page every stitch is up for ripping my dream never leaves me the laid blue wool shining buttons slim silver needles I recognize the elegance of materials just as they are untouched at the threshold of a room though I cannot see outward nor for whom I hold the materials I am ready;

WHEREAS *re-*

solution's an act

of analyzing and re-

structuring complex

ideas into simpler

ones so I place

a black bracket

on either side of

an [idea] I cordon it

to safety away

from national re-

solution the threat

of re-

ductive

[thinking]:

Hermaneutic: tool that teaches
you how to use something

look on pg 85
things taken away – to safety away
shielding them

Whereas Native Peoples are [   ] people with a deep and abiding [   ] in the [   ], and for millennia Native Peoples have maintained a powerful [   ] connection to this land, as evidenced by their [   ] and legends;

•

Whereas the Federal Government condemned the [   ], [   ], and [   ] of Native Peoples and endeavored to assimilate them by such policies as the redistribution of land under the Act of February 8, 1887 (25 U.S.C. 331; 24 Stat. 388, chapter 119) (commonly known as the "General Allotment Act"), and the forcible removal of Native [   ] from their [   ] to faraway boarding schools where their Native [   ] and [   ] were degraded and forbidden;

WHEREAS I read an article in the *New York Times* about the federal sequestration of funds from reservation programs, the cuts. In federal promises and treaties. The article details living conditions on reservations a suicide rate ten times higher than the rest of the country. Therein the story of a twelve-year-old girl whose mother died, she doesn't know her father, she bounces home to home to foster home, weary. I regard how plainly the writer imparts her repeated sexual abuse. For mental care, unavailable services. There's a clinic that doesn't have money after May, *don't get sick after May* is the important message. As I read I cry, I always cry, and here I must be clear my crying doesn't indicate sadness. Then I read a comment posted below the online article:

> *I am a fourteen-year-old girl who recently visited the _____ Reservation in South Dakota, with my youth group. The conditions the Native American people were living in were shocking. When I arrived home, I wrote a petition on whitehouse.gov for the US to formally apologize and pay reparations to the Native American people. This petition only stays up until July 23rd, so please sign and share!!! You signing it would really mean a lot to a lot of people. Thank you.*

Dear Fourteen-Year-Old Girl, I want to write. The government has already "formally apologized" to Native American people on behalf of the plural *you,* your youth group, your mother and father, your best friends and their families. *You,* as in all American citizens. *You* didn't know that, I know. Yet indeed, Dear Girl, the conditions on reservations have changed since the Apology. Meaning, the Apology has been followed by budget sequestration. In common terms sequestration is removal banishment or exile. In law-speak it means seizure for safekeeping but changed in federal budgeting to mean subject to cuts, best as I can understand it. Dear Girl, I went to the Indian Health Services to fix a tooth, a complicated pain. Indian health care is guaranteed by treaty but at the clinic limited funds don't allow treatment beyond a filling. The solution offered: *Pull it.* Under pliers masks and clinical lights, a tooth that could've been saved was placed in my palm to hold after sequestration. Dear Girl, I honor your response and action, I do. Yet the root of reparation is repair. My tooth will not grow back. The root, gone.

[spiritual]

[belief]   [Creator]

[spiritual]

[customs]

[traditions]

[beliefs]   [customs]

[children]   [families]

[practices]

[languages]

(2) Resolutions

(1)

I recognize

the special legal and
political relationship
Indian tribes have with
the United States and

the solemn

covenant with the land
we share.

(2)

I

commend   this land

and   this   land

honor   this   land

Native   this   land

Peoples   ☐   this land

for   this   land

the   this   land

thousands this   land

of   this   land

years   this   land

that   this land

they   this   land

have   this   land

stewarded   this   land

and   this   land

protected this land this land this land this land this land this land this

                                    this

(3)

I

recognize

that [1]

official [2]

ill- [3]

breaking of [4]

the [5]

Indian [6]

---

1. *there have been years of* 2. *depradations,* 3. *conceived policies, and the* 4. *covenants by*
5. *Federal Government regarding* 6. *tribes*

(4) I have thought carefully about certain terms in English, the language in which the Apology is written. Likewise, since the Apology is issued to Native people, I have considered Native languages. For months, I dwelled on the word "apologizes." As you may already know, in many Native languages, there is no word for "apologize." The same goes for "sorry." This doesn't mean that in Native communities where the word "apologize" is not spoken, there aren't definite actions for admitting and amending wrongdoing. Thus, I wonder how, without the word, this text translates as a gesture—

> The United States, acting through Congress— ▉▉▉▉▉ on behalf of the people of the United States to all Native Peoples for the many instances of violence, maltreatment, and neglect inflicted on Native Peoples by citizens of the United States;

(5) *I express commitment to reveal in a text the shape of its pounding—*

 e x p r e s s e s i t s
 r e g r e t
 f o r t h e
 r a m i f i
c a t i o n s o f f o r m e r w r o n g s a n d i t s c o m m i t m e n t t o b u i l d o n t h
e p o s i t i v e r e l a t i o n s h i p s o f t h e p a s t a n d p r e s e n t t o m o v e t o w a
r d a b r i g h t e r f u t u r e w h e r e a l l t h e p e o p l e o f t h i s l a n d l i v e r e c o n
c i l e d a s b r o t h e r s a n d s i s t e r s a n d h a r m o n i o u s l y s t e w a r d a n
 d p r o t
 e c t t h
 i s l a n d t
 o g e t h e r

(6) *I too urge the President to acknowledge the wrongs of the United States against Indian tribes in the history of the United States in order to bring healing to this land although healing this land is not dependent never has been upon this President meaning tribal nations and the people themselves are healing this land its waters with or without Presidential acknowledgment they act upon this right without apology—*

To speak to law enforcement

these Direct Action Principles

be really clear always ask

have been painstakingly drafted

who what when where why

at behest of the local leadership

e.g. Officer, my name is _____

from Standing Rock

please explain

and are the guidelines

the probable cause for stopping me

for the Očhéthi Šakówiŋ camp

you may ask

I acknowledge a plurality of ways

does that seem reasonable to you

to resist oppression

don't give any further info

•

                                        People ask why do you bring up

we are Protectors

                        so many other issues it's because

we are peaceful & prayerful

                                these issues have been ongoing

"isms" have no place

                        for 200 years they're interdependent

here we all stand together

                                        we teach the distinction

we are non-violent

                                btwn civil rights & civil liberties

we are proud to stand

                                btwn what's legal & what isn't legal

no masks

                                        the camp is 100% volunteer

respect locals

                                it's a choice to be a Protector

no weapons

                                        liberty is freedom

or what could be construed as weapons

                                        of speech it's a right

property damage does not get us closer

                                        to privacy a fair trial

to our goal

                                        you're free

all campers must get an orientation

                                        from unreasonable search

Direct Action Training

                                        free from seizure of person or home

is required

                                        & civil disobedience: the camp is

for everyone taking action

                                        an act of civil disobedience

no children

                                        now the law protects the corporation

in potentially dangerous situations

                                        so the camp is illegal

we keep each accountable

                                        you must have a buddy system

to these principles

                                        someone must know when you're leaving

this is a ceremony

                                        & when you're coming back

act accordingly

(7) I commend the inventive crafting of a national resolution so mindful of—

boundaries

their boundaries

in their boundaries

located in their boundaries

tribes located in their boundaries

Indian tribes located in their boundaries

recognized Indian tribes located in their boundaries

with recognized Indian tribes located in their boundaries

efforts with recognized Indian tribes located in their boundaries

reconciliation efforts with recognized Indian tribes located in their

begun reconciliation efforts with recognized Indian tribes located in

have begun reconciliation efforts with recognized Indian tribes located

that have begun reconciliation efforts with recognized Indian tribes

governments that have begun reconciliation efforts with recognized Indian

State governments that have begun reconciliation efforts with recognized

the State governments that have begun reconciliation efforts with

commends the State governments that have begun reconciliation efforts

boundaries

their boundaries

in their boundaries

located in their boundaries

tribes located in their boundaries

Indiantribeslocatedintheirboundaries

recognizedIndiantribeslocatedintheirboundaries

withrecognizedIndiantribeslocatedintheirboundaries

(3) Disclaimer

Nothing in this book—

(1) authorizes or supports any claim against Layli Long Soldier by the United States; or

(2) serves as a settlement of any claim against Layli Long Soldier by the United States, here in   the grassesgrassesgrasses.

Notes

"Diction":

In the third part of the poem, the lifted paragraph is from Zitkála Šá's "Impressions of an Indian Childhood," in her chapter titled "The Beadwork," found in *American Indian Stories,* originally published by Hayworth Publishing House, 1921. In the fourth part of the poem, the corner arrangement is from page 147 of James Welch's *Killing Custer: The Battle of the Little Bighorn and the Fate of the Plains Indians,* published by W. W. Norton & Company, 1994.

"WHEREAS":

The Congressional Resolution of Apology to Native Americans (S. J. Res. 14—111th Congress (2009–2010)) is available online at: congress.gov.

In the thirteenth "Whereas Statement" ("WHEREAS her birth signaled . . ."), the philosopher writing about his mother is Jacques Derrida, and the quoted lines are from his "Circumfession by Jacques Derrida," found in *Jacques Derrida* by Geoffrey Bennington and Jacques Derrida, published by the University of Chicago Press, 1993.

In the twentieth "Whereas Statement" ("WHEREAS I read an article . . ."), the article referenced is "Broken Promises" by Byron L. Dorgan, from the *New York Times,* July 10, 2013. The comment by the fourteen-year-old girl is viewable in the online edition of the article.

In the sixth "Resolution" ("I too urge the President . . ."), following the opening paragraph, the text at left is from Mark K. Tilsen (Pine Ridge, South Dakota) in his Facebook post, September 20, 2016; the text at right is from Waniya Locke (Standing Rock, North Dakota) in a personal interview conducted by the author, September 19, 2016.

Acknowledgments

Thank you and love to my mother, Loevia Hockley, who has helped with childcare, meals, and housework to see this manuscript through; and more than anything, for your rock of stability and wisdom. Thank you to my father, Daniel Long Soldier, for showing me that we can grow, change, and make peace with ourselves and others; for your constant admonition to *be humble, be humble* and to persevere. Tightest hugs of gratitude around my daughter, Chance Ohitika Alexie White—who appears in so many of these poems—for her bright energy and the sense of purpose she has given me. Thank you to Chance's father, Orlando White, for the many conversations and support in the making of these poems. Thank you to Auntie Tilda Long Soldier St. Pierre and Uncle Mark St. Pierre for allowing me to spend time on your land, which inspired me to write about grassesgrassesgrasses. Thank you to *all* of my Long Soldier and Hockley relatives. I could not have written these poems without the grounding and voices of my family.

Thank you to faculty, staff, and peers at the Institute of American Indian Arts who helped form my interests in poetry—and most especially the concerns of Native literature. You are my foundation. I especially thank Arthur Sze, John Davis, James Thomas Stevens, Sherwin Bitsui, dg nanouk okpik, Jennifer Elise Foerster, Erika T. Wurth, Evelina Zuni Lucero, and Mark Turcotte for your inspiration, critique, and/or counsel over the years.

Thank you, also, to faculty, visiting artists, staff, and peers at Bard College's Milton Avery Graduate School of the Arts for opening me up to a world of possibilities. My first two years at Bard, I could barely speak a word in group settings. Yet I left with the framework for *WHEREAS,* that is, itself, a gesture of speaking back. Very special thanks to Arthur Gibbons, Ann Lauterbach, Anselm Berrigan, Anna Moschovakis, Renee Gladman, Matvei Yankelevich, David Levi Strauss, Robert Fitterman, Tracie Morris, Jeanne Liotta, Taylor Davis, Zoe Leonard, Fia Backström, Matana Roberts, Barbara Ess, Kenji Fujita, Harry Dodge, Malik Gaines, and Alex Segade for memorable insights that contributed to this work. I thank my Bard friends who sat on the ledges and shared in this labor of thought—Yasamin Ghiasi, Greyson Hong, Lily Gottlieb-McHale, Aykan Safoğlu, Leyna Papach, Gilda Davidian, Krista Belle Stewart, Nathan Young, Alex Cuff, Mirene Arsanios, Will Heinrich, Daisy Atterbury, Genji Amino, Jessica Millnitz, and Camonghne Felix.

A heartfelt thank you to my sister-friend and collaborator Mary Bordeaux, former curator at the Heritage Center at Red Cloud Indian School, for helping to organize *Whereas We Respond,* a three-month interactive installation wherein the community of Pine Ridge Reservation responded to the Congressional Resolution of Apology to Native Americans. Special thank yous, as well, to Mary Maxon, Ashley Pourier, and the Red Cloud Indian School for their support of this installation.

Warmest gratitude to faculty and staff at Naropa University's Jack Kerouac School of Disembodied Poetics for your belief in my work—dating back to my undergraduate studies in the Summer Writing Program. Endless thank yous to Anne Waldman, Eleni Sikelianos, and Laird Hunt for continual support, inspiration, and inclusion. My touchstones.

Thank you to Q Avenue Press for your publication of my first chapbook of poems, *Chromosomory,* which was a gale of wind to set me toward writing poems in Part I of *WHEREAS.* True gratitude to Curtis Bauer, Sebastian Matthews, and Ross Gay.

Thank you to Waniya Locke, Mark K. Tilsen, and Dan Namingha for your time and personal correspondence that helped me complete pieces that are so dear to me.

Thank you to Mona Susan Power for the close reading of "38." It meant the world to me to receive your feedback on aspects of craft as well as Dakota perspective and history.

Thank you to the Lannan Foundation for your unbelievable generosity—both financial and with a writing residency in Marfa, Texas, for the completion of this book. My warmest embrace around Martha Jessup for her listening ear and gentle coordination of the "practical things." And to Patrick Lannan and the Lannan family—your support of the literary community and writers like me is profound and important. Thank you all so very much.

Thank you to the Native Arts and Culture Foundation for the Artist Fellowship during the arduous and silent stages of revising *WHEREAS.* Your excitement strengthened me to continue. Francene J. Blythe, thank you for our meeting filled with art talk and, most importantly, life talk! I sincerely appreciate the work that NACF does for Native artists.

Thank you to the Whiting Foundation for financial support, much-needed financial counsel, and the invitation to share my work in New York. A personal thank you to Courtney Hodell for the coordination of so many details and for your warm welcome.

Thank you to Duane Linklater and Brian Jungen for the cover photograph on this book. And a bow of gratitude to Duane and Tanya Lukin Linklater for your friendship, vision, and valuable critical responses in the development of these poems.

Thank you, Joy Harjo, my literary auntie, for your generous words and encouragement over the years. Maggie Nelson, thank you for inviting me to submit to *PEN America* and for taking an interest in *WHEREAS* in its beginning stages. And Fred Moten, so deeply, I thank you for your kindness and intellectual tenacity. I will always remember your delight in "languageness." There are pedestals in my heart for all of you.

Immense gratitude to Jeff Shotts for your keen eye, openness, and gentle suggestions in all aspects of making *WHEREAS.* Thank you for your invitation to see more of my work, years ago, when you and Steve Woodward first read "Ḣe Sápa." That invitation led to this book with Graywolf, which I am utterly grateful to be able to share with others.

Finally, sincere thank yous to the following literary journals and online sites for first publishing these poems:

The Academy of American Poets Poem-A-Day for "Irony";

Ahani: Indigenous American Poetry for "Wakȟályapi";

American Indian Culture and Research Journal for "Diction";

The American Poetry Review for "Dilate" and "Left";

American Poets for "Whereas a Friend Senses";

The American Reader for "Whereas I Query My Uneasiness";

As/Us for "Talent";

The Brooklyn Rail for "Vaporative";

Denver Quarterly for "Waȟpánič̌a," formerly titled "Atontansni," and for "Resolution (1)," Resolution (2)," "Resolution (3)," and "Resolution (4)";

Eleven Eleven: A Journal of Literature & Art for "Now Make Room" and "Steady Summer";

The Kenyon Review Online for "Ȟe Sápa";

Lit Hub for "Resolution (5)," "Resolution (6)," and "Resolution (7)";

Mud City Journal for "38";

Orion for "Whereas I Did Not Desire in Childhood";

PEN America: A Journal for Writers and Readers and *The Land We Are: Artists and Writers Unsettle the Politics of Reconciliation* for "Whereas My Eyes Land," "Whereas I Tire," "Whereas Her Birth," "Whereas I Sipped Winter Water," and "Whereas I Read an Article";

Poetry for "Whereas a String-Bean Blue-Eyed Man," "Whereas We Ride to the Airport," "Whereas a Woman I Know," and "Whereas the Word *Whereas*";

Sing: Poetry from the Indigenous Americas (University of Arizona Press) for "Dilate" and "Wakȟályapi";

Talking Stick Native Arts Quarterly for "Edge" and "Tókȟah'aŋ";

Taos Journal of International Poetry & Art for "We" and "Head Count";

THEthe Poetry for "Let," formerly titled "This";

Toad for "Left"

LAYLI LONG SOLDIER holds a BFA from the Institute of American Indian Arts and an MFA from Bard College. She has served as a contributing editor of *Drunken Boat*. Her poems have appeared in the *American Poetry Review, American Poets,* the *American Reader,* the *Kenyon Review Online, Poetry,* and other publications. She is the recipient of a 2015 Native Arts and Cultures Foundation National Artist Fellowship, a 2015 Lannan Literary Fellowship, and a 2016 Whiting Award. She lives in Santa Fe, New Mexico.

The text of *WHEREAS* is set in Adobe Garamond Pro. Book design by Rachel Holscher. Composition by Bookmobile Design and Digital Publisher Services, Minneapolis, Minnesota. Manufactured by Versa Press on acid-free, 30 percent postconsumer wastepaper.